A Change

by Tom Sato
illustrated by Liz Callen

Practice Decodable 54

I0806547

McGraw Hill Education

Bothell, WA • Chicago, IL • Columbus, OH • New York, NY

MHEonline.com

Send all inquiries to:
McGraw-Hill Education
8787 Orion Place
Columbus, OH 43240

ISBN: 978-0-02-145611-6
MHID: 0-02-145611-9

Printed in China

8 9 10 11 12 DSS 27 26 25 24 23

The gingerbread man is on this page.
He yells, "Catch up if you can!"

On stage, I am the gingerbread man.
I am larger.

On the page, the gingerbread man has to go past animals.

A fox tricks the gingerbread man.

It can catch the gentle gingerbread man.

On stage, we change that.
I see the danger of the fox.

The gingerbread man runs and runs.
I am glad.